DEDICATION

For Rob and Sadie with love, as always.

100

THINGS TO DO ON

CAPE COD
AND THE ISLANDS
BEFORE YOU
DIE

100

THINGS TO DO ON
CAPE COD
AND THE ISLANDS
BEFORE YOU
DIE

· ·

KIM FOLEY MACKINNON

REEDY PRESS

Library of Congress Control Number: 2021950828

ISBN: 9781681063478

Design by Jill Halpin

All photos by the author unless otherwise noted.

Printed in the United States of America
22 23 24 25 26   5 4 3 2 1

CONTENTS

• •

Music and Entertainment

Culture and History

Shopping and Fashion

PREFACE

Massachusetts is famous for many things, but as residents of the Bay State know, one of its most special regions is composed of Cape Cod, Martha's Vineyard, and Nantucket. The Cape, a crescent of land shaped like an elbow stretching 90 miles into the Atlantic Ocean, is dotted with quaint seaside villages. Martha's Vineyard and Nantucket, islands to the south of the Cape, each have unique histories, attractions, and landscapes.

Trying to capture just 100 things about the Cape and islands to feature in this book was a rather daunting task, as there is so much more to these famous vacation playgrounds than beaches, lighthouses, and clam shacks (though those are all great!). I could easily have doubled the number of entries and still not reavealed all there is to see and do.

Fascinating museums, world-class art, outstanding restaurants, miles of trails, and natural beauty await travelers year-round on the Cape and islands. Exploring Cape Cod by car and meandering through each of its small towns to discover something new is always an adventure. And while you can fly to Martha's Vineyard or Nantucket, I'd never trade the slower ferry for that mode of transportation. Once aboard and en route to either island, I feel like I'm already free of my mainland cares.

I'd love to hear about your experiences with my picks, and I'd especially welcome your ideas and discoveries! Look for me on Instagram and Twitter @escapewithkim, and tag your own Cape Cod and island adventures at #100ThingsCape&Islands.

• •

ACKNOWLEDGMENTS

All books are a collaboration and not the work of just one person. I owe a big thank you to all my friends and family whom I hit up for ideas, who offer me advice and encouragement, and who love to help me with researching where to eat and drink! I am also fortunate enough to have worked with many outstanding public relations people over the years, and I especially want to thank William "Bill" De Sousa, who is always unfailingly helpful and gracious. Last but not least, I have to say thank you to Josh Stevens and everyone at Reedy Press for their support (and patience) over the years, especially in 2020. It's always a pleasure and an honor to work with you.

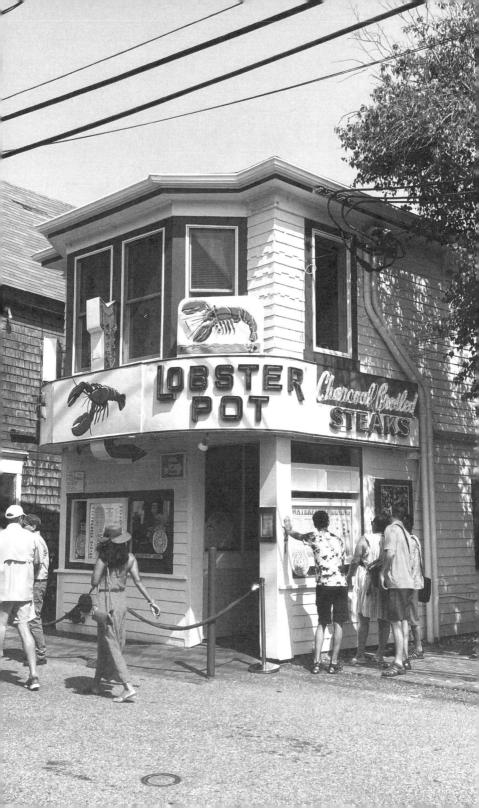

FOOD AND DRINK

SET YOUR SIGHTS
ON THE PILOT HOUSE

If the views don't win you over, classics like clam chowder, baked stuffed lobster, and fried clams probably will at this seafood-focused restaurant located on the Sandwich Marina on the Cape Cod Canal. This casual and lively spot is a popular seasonal restaurant and quite reasonably priced for the Cape. Though the menu is definitely seafood-forward, carnivores and vegetarians will find plenty to eat, with steak tips, ribs, and veggie burgers, vegan bowls, and salads available. It's also usually possible to snag a table at the large restaurant, which has indoor and outdoor seating. Live music makes for a festive atmosphere. The Pilot House is a three-minute walk from the Cape Cod Canal Visitor Center (page 86).

14 Gallo Rd., Sandwich, 508-888-8889
pilothousecapecod.com

DOWN A DOZEN
AT NAKED OYSTER BISTRO

This French/seafood bistro serves up delicious oysters from its own farm in nearby Barnstable. Oyster lovers will find about two dozen raw or "dressed" oyster dishes served any number of ways, from "naked" to oysters Rockefeller. Chef and owner Florence Lowell is passionate about serving local products and works with farmers and anglers in the region to that end. Seafood, caught hours before, is often brought directly from the ocean to the kitchen to be served that same day. Classic French bistro fare, such as duck confit and country pâté, along with lobster orzo and sirloin steak, round out the menu. Creative cocktails, including the Naked Cantaloupe and the Black Fig, are fun to try.

410 Main St., Hyannis, 508-778-6500
nakedoyster.com

ENJOY THE VIEW
AT OCEAN HOUSE

Located in an unbelievably scenic spot on Nantucket Sound on the coast of Dennis, the Ocean House Restaurant, located at the Three Seasons Resort, offers an upscale experience with a creative menu and a surprising number of offerings for vegetarians. Dishes such as General Gao's cauliflower, zucchini and sweet pepper fritters, and mushroom risotto are all stars, not afterthoughts. The popular Cape Cod Potato Chip–crusted fish and chips and Korean braised short ribs are also big crowd-pleasers. Even the dessert menu is thoughtful, with a vegan dark cherry cheesecake and gluten-free brownie sundae. The dining room overlooks the water, and even if you don't get a window table, the views are lovely. There's also outdoor seating and a beach bar.

425 Old Wharf Rd., Dennis Port, 508-394-0700
oceanhouserestaurant.com

BE TRANSPORTED
AT BUCA'S TUSCAN ROADHOUSE

This Italian restaurant offers a taste of Tuscany on the Cape, with a menu bursting with Italian favorites such as arancini, Bolognese pasta, and veal scallopini, plus a long wine list filled with Super Tuscans and Chiantis. If you are looking for a romantic spot for dinner, look no further. Twinkling lights and red-and-white checked tablecloths set a cozy scene. The owners say they want to transport you to a tiny town called Greve in the Chianti region of Italy. As a person who has actually been to the charming town of Greve, I can confirm that they have done an excellent job in that department.

4 Depot Rd., Harwich, 508-432-6900
bucastuscanroadhouse.com

CHECK OUT CHILLINGSWORTH

The "Best of Dining" lists about the Cape, from cuisine to romantic to elegant, almost always include Chillingsworth, and with good reason. Located on the 300-year-old Chillingsworth Foster estate in Brewster, the fine dining restaurant offers a French menu paired with outstanding service. For many, this is their go-to special occasion spot, but you don't need a birthday or anniversary to enjoy tuna tartare, escargot, roasted duck breast, and other exquisitely made dishes. The more casual Chill's Bistro offers dishes such as truffle mac and cheese and steamed mussels.

2449 Main St., Brewster, 508-896-3640
chillingsworth.com

TIP

There are also three guest rooms located
bove the restaurant if you want to make
a weekend of it.

SATE YOUR SUSHI CRAVINGS
AT MAC'S SHACK

When writing about Mac's seafood restaurants, it's difficult to focus on just one place—there are several restaurants and markets scattered around the Cape—but the Mac's brand is strictly a local chain (though it does ship across the country) owned and operated by a local fisherman's family. Mac's Shack in Wellfleet is known for its excellent and extensive sushi menu, fun outdoor bar, and lively atmosphere. It goes without saying that seafood is the specialty at Mac's, so if you don't fill up on sushi (ask for the specials of the day, which are always excellent), you can order entrees such as broiled scallops and steamed lobsters.

91 Commercial St., Wellfleet, 508-349-6333
macsseafood.com

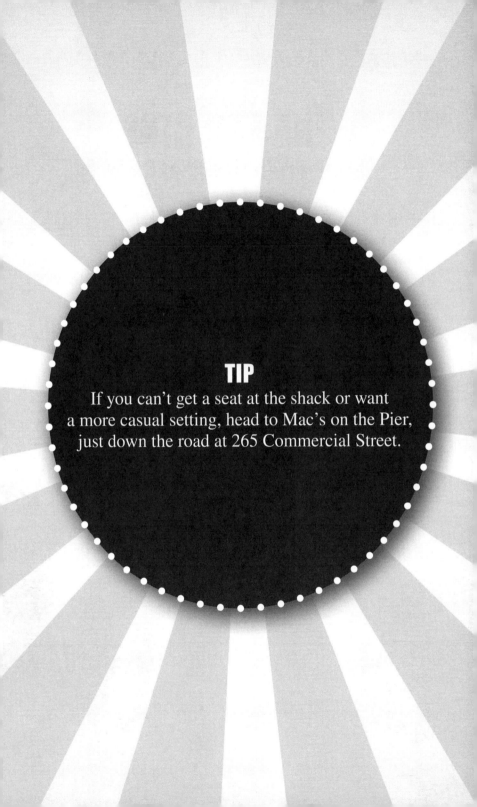

TIP

If you can't get a seat at the shack or want a more casual setting, head to Mac's on the Pier, just down the road at 265 Commercial Street.

WINE AND DINE
AT WICKED OYSTER

Located in a charming 18th-century former home, Wicked Oyster is a destination dining spot for those who love the great service and dishes like tuna sashimi, chopped clam pizza, "lazy" lobster, and grilled fish. Weekly specials take advantage of the local catch. Burgers and steaks will please those who don't prefer seafood. If you like any of the art on the walls, made by local artists, ask about it. Pieces are from the Berta Walker Gallery in Provincetown, and most are available to buy. The restaurant is also open on weekends for breakfast, with omelets made to order, a variety of Benedict dishes, and other morning favorites.

50 Main St., Wellfleet, 508-349-3455
thewickedo.com

VIVE LA FRANCE
AT PB BOULANGERIE

You might not expect to find an outstanding French bakery in Wellfleet, let alone one that people swear would be at home in Paris, but PB Boulangerie manages to pull it off. It has practically a cult following, and people line up in the mornings to get a freshly baked croissant, *pain au chocolat*, or fruit danish, all of which are almost too beautiful to eat. Other treats include cream puffs, macaroons, and meringues. And don't forget to buy a loaf of bread! Baguettes, *bâtards*, and *boules* fly out of the bakery. Lunch options include soup of the day and sandwiches served on baguettes. Prepared classics, such as escargot, pâté, and beef bourguignon, are available to go so you can re-create your own corner of France at home.

15 LeCount Hollow Rd., South Wellfleet, 508-349-1600
pbboulangeriebistro.com

LOVE LOBSTER
AT THE LOBSTER POT

Since 1979, this iconic corner spot with its bright neon lobster sign has been a lure to anyone walking down Commercial Street. While a tourist might mistake this for a typical gimmicky spot, locals know better and will tell you so. If you want to go full bore with lobster, start with the lobster avocado appetizer, then try the lobster egg roll, and finally order a main dish of boiled or baked lobster with all the fixings. Other specialties include seafood paella, BBQ pepper shrimp, and Portuguese fish. But it's not all seafood. The extensive menu offers everything from chicken to steaks to vegetarian choices. While you may have to wait to get a table (no reservations accepted), it's worth it.

321 Commercial St., Provincetown, 508-487-0842
ptownlobsterpot.com

PICK UP A PINT
AT PROVINCETOWN BREWING CO.

The Provincetown Brewing Co. taproom, located in the heart of Provincetown, opened in 2019 and serves up a side of activism with its brews. All the company's products highlight a cause or organization, from LGBTQ+ rights to conservation, and a percentage of its sales is donated to various charities. Whether that's important to you or not, the beers are quite tasty, and the atmosphere is fun. There are comfy couches, a pool table, and a big bar inside, plus a dog-friendly patio outside. Beer selections include the Bearded Mistress IPA, Golden Hook Ale, and Crandaddy Sour, along with seasonal offerings; the food menu includes a variety of sandwiches, salads, and shareable plates like nachos and a Mediterranean platter with hummus, olives, and pita.

141 Bradford St., Provincetown, 508-413-9076
provincetownbrewingco.com

GET A BITE
AT BLACK DOG TAVERN

If you haven't yet seen the ubiquitous Black Dog logo, popular on T-shirts, coffee mugs, and beach towels in Massachusetts and around the world, once you arrive on the island, you certainly will. The story goes that a little over 50 years ago, Captain Robert Douglas, unhappy with the lack of good year-round restaurants on the island, opened his own and named it after his dog. Now Black Dog is practically an industry unto itself, with numerous outposts and retail outlets. You can even take a sail on the Black Dog's schooner. The main restaurant in Vineyard Haven still serves up favorites like clam chowder, lobster rolls, and crab cakes. Snag a table by the windows for lovely views.

20 Beach St., Vineyard Haven, 508-693-9223
theblackdog.com/pages/the-black-dog-tavern

SOAK IN SOME HISTORY
AT NEWES FROM AMERICA PUB

This classic British-style pub in the basement of a historic 18th-century hotel in Edgartown just oozes atmosphere. It's fun to grab a pint and enjoy classic fare like fish and chips (or the addictive onion rings) any time of year, but it's especially cozy in the winter when there's a fire blazing away in the central fireplace. If you see nameplates on the back of bar stools or patrons asking for their personalized mugs, they earned that distinction by buying beers and collecting wooden nickels. After a certain amount, you can gain your own claim to fame, though it might take a while—certainly longer than one vacation!

23 Kelly St., Edgartown, 508-627-4397
thekelleyhousehotel.com/restaurant/newes-pub

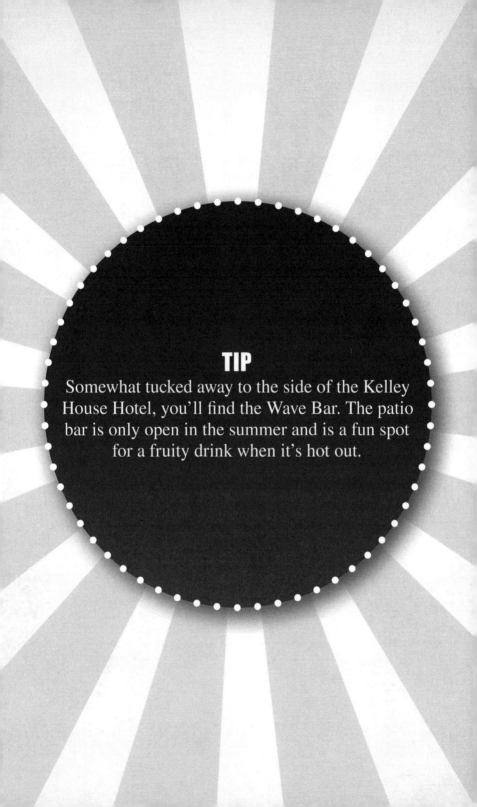

TIP

Somewhat tucked away to the side of the Kelley House Hotel, you'll find the Wave Bar. The patio bar is only open in the summer and is a fun spot for a fruity drink when it's hot out.

TOSS SOME PEANUT SHELLS
AT OFFSHORE ALE COMPANY

When you take your seat at Offshore Ale, you get a complimentary basket of peanuts and are told to simply throw the shells on the floor after shucking them. It may be unorthodox, but it's fun, especially for kids. Just don't eat too many before your meal arrives. You don't want to be too full to eat your lobster roll, fish and chips, or one of the signature wood-fired pizzas. (I recommend the outstanding mashed potato, cheddar cheese, bacon, and scallion one!) Offshore also brews delicious craft beers—it was the first brewpub on the island—and has a rotating list available, with favorites like East Chop Lighthouse golden ale and the flagship Amber Ale on tap. Fortunately for locals and off-season visitors, the restaurant stays open year-round.

30 Kennebec Ave., Oak Bluffs, 508-693-2626
offshoreale.com

ORDER A SLICE
AT GIORDANO'S

Serving pizzas and Italian food since 1930, this family-run restaurant, now with the fourth generation in charge of things, is an Oak Bluffs institution. Does the season even start until it opens? It's an open question. You can dine inside or grab a slice at the to-go window and take it to the beach. Even if my family is just getting pizza, we are incapable of starting our meal without an order or two of the garlic bread with mozzarella cheese, a.k.a. "cheesy bread." That said, we almost always order the Neapolitan-style pizza because, why wouldn't we? Occasionally, though, we do stray to something like chicken parm or meatballs and spaghetti, and it's all as comforting as it sounds.

18 Lake Ave., Oak Bluffs, 508-693-0184
giosmv.com

TIP

Gio's doesn't take reservations, so be prepared to wait in line during the busy season.

GET A LOBSTER ROLL
AT LARSEN'S FISH MARKET

This is my favorite place in all the world to get a lobster roll. There's nothing like visiting on a gorgeous summer's day, watching as a freshly caught lobster is plucked out of the cooking pot and picked in front of you, and then loaded onto a hot dog roll and doused in butter. Taking it out back and sitting on an old trap to eat it is one of the great pleasures of life, as far as I am concerned. A first-time visitor to the small fishing village of Menemsha might not guess at this experience looking at Larsen's from the outside, but now you know! You can also get all sorts of fresh fish to cook at home, if you can wait that long. If you prefer to dine while watching the sunset from the beach, you can also get whole steamed lobsters, freshly shucked oysters, crab cakes, and more from the small kitchen. Just BYOB and a blanket.

56 Basin Rd., Chilmark, 508-645-2680
larsensfishmarket.com

DOWN A BREW
AT BAD MARTHA FARMER'S BREWERY

Head to Donaroma's Nursery and you'll find the Bad Martha brewery in a lovely setting, open from May through October (and during Christmas). Opened in 2014, the brewery offers a rotating slate of beers, from Vineyard Summer Ale to Oyster Stout, and while it tries to keep 10 varieties on tap, popular ones often sell out quickly. You can also get a free sample to see what you like or opt for a flight to taste more than one. If you're hungry, cheese, veggie, or charcuterie plates and pizzas are on offer. Outdoor games (such as cornhole) and local bands are a feature on weekends. There's also a second location in Falmouth, open year-round, for those who want to grab a beer on the mainland off-season.

Martha's Vineyard
270 Upper Main St., Edgartown, 508-939-4415

Cape Cod
876 E Falmouth Hwy., Falmouth, 508-372-6740

badmarthabeer.com/brewery

SWIZZLE A RUM
AT NOMANS

This lively and fun spot is especially enjoyable on a sunny day when you can sit outside on the expansive lawn and play a game of cornhole or Jenga while sipping a signature house-made rum cocktail. Nomans is named after a 628-acre rock of the same name three miles off the coast of the Vineyard, said to have been used by rumrunners during Prohibition. The restaurant offers two house rums, one a blend of 8- and 13-year-old dark rums, and one a light rum aged for three years (both produced at the Triple Eight Distillery on Nantucket). As for food, the menu features a number of surprisingly creative and delicious vegetarian dishes, such as mushroom tacos and falafel burgers, but carnivores and seafood lovers are covered too, with fish tacos, lobster rolls, cheeseburgers, and more.

15 Island Inn Rd., Oak Bluffs, 508-338-2474
nomansmv.com

GO BACK
TO BACK DOOR DONUTS

Martha's Vineyard isn't exactly a late-night hot spot. Don't get me wrong, some bars and clubs stay open late, but if you want a bite, you're usually out of luck—except for this special spot that can cure your sugary cravings until midnight or 1 a.m. on the weekends. By day, the Front Bakery Café serves up regular bakery items, but at night, busy bakers serve up freshly made donuts by the dozens. The line can easily wrap around the block on a hot summer's night, but no one ever minds. It's always a festive atmosphere. I'm a glazed donut kind of person, but I have been known to share one of the delicious apple fritters on occasion.

1-11 Kennebec Ave., Oak Bluffs, 508-693-3688
backdoordonuts.com

SLURP AN OYSTER
AT TOPPER'S

Topper's, located in the upscale and remote Wauwinet resort about 20 minutes outside of town, faces the Nantucket Bay on one side and the Atlantic Ocean on the other. Sunset at the restaurant is a special treat, and pairing it with locally harvested Retsyo oysters, which are cultivated and harvested just 300 yards from the restaurant, is always a great idea. Topper's usually offers tasting menus, with an expected focus on fresh seafood and local produce, and optional wine pairings. And the well-stocked wine cellar offers about 1,500 wines. In warm weather, dining on the deck is a must.

120 Wauwinet Rd., 508-228-8768
wauwinet.com/dining

OPT FOR ORIGINAL
AT ÒRAN MÓR

This is an island favorite, located on the second floor of a historic building (book early if you want an outdoor balcony table) and often recognized for its excellent service. The restaurant celebrates different cuisines and cultures with finesse, so you might order the Moroccan fish tagine with the day's market catch, Long Island duck breast with a honey glaze, or bison au poivre, depending on your mood. If you lean more toward pasta, options might include lobster gemelli or black truffle bucatini. Whatever you order, it is sure to be creative and delicious. The Mórtini, the restaurant's signature cocktail, is composed of gin, white vermouth, and lemon and is often the first thing repeat diners order. Wrap up your meal with fresh madeleines à la minute.

2 S Beach St., 508-228-8655
oranmorbistro.com

SET SAIL FOR A MEAL
AT STRAIGHT WHARF

For almost 50 years, Straight Wharf has been a favorite dining destination for countless patrons, with an elegant ambiance and excellent service. The menu changes nightly so the chef can present the freshest in-season ingredients. Starters might include a personal clam bake with littleneck clams, butter-poached lobster, spicy chorizo sausage, fingerling potatoes, and corn. Entrees might include day boat scallops with grapefruit, fennel, endive, kumquat, and watercress, or chicken under a brick with grilled romaine. Start your meal with a signature cocktail, such as a Swagger Like Us (bourbon, Aperol, Averna, and grapefruit), and end with tasty dessert such as an olive oil cake or espresso panna cotta.

6 Harbor Square, 508-228-4499
straightwharfrestaurant.com

GET FISHY
AT 167 RAW NANTUCKET

While it began as a fish market in 1978, 167 Raw Nantucket is so much more today, showcasing fresh seafood, of course, but also offering prime meats, fine cheeses, wine and beer, and gourmet items for sale in the market. There's also a food truck on the property. It's an awesome spot for a casual meal, with delicious lobster rolls, fish tacos, fried fish sandwiches, ceviche, and more. You can enjoy your meal and anything else you pick up at the market in the garden, which has plenty of seating. The market also operates a raw bar at Cisco Brewers, with raw oysters, littleneck clams, shrimp cocktail, and the like. Should you find yourself down south, there's an outpost of the oyster bar, as well as a sushi bar, in Charleston, South Carolina.

167 Hummock Pond Rd., 508-228-2871
167raw.com

SIP SUDS
AT CISCO BREWERS

Founded near Cisco Beach in 1995, Cisco Brewers quickly grew into a wildly popular brand. Today you'll find the brewery alongside Nantucket Vineyards and the Triple Eight Distillery, which makes a variety of liquors. The outdoor beer garden often has food trucks and live music, so you can eat and be entertained too. Beers you might recognize include the Whale's Tale pale ale, Coastal Getaway IPA, and Grey Lady wheat ale. Check the brewery's website for tours. Cisco Brewers also operates a brewery and taproom in Portsmouth, New Hampshire, and a seasonal pop-up beer garden in Boston.

5 Bartlett Farm Rd., 508-325-5929
ciscobrewers.com

MUSIC
AND ENTERTAINMENT

SEE A SHOW
AT THE CAPE PLAYHOUSE

When an actor takes the stage at the Cape Playhouse in Dennis, the "longest-running professional summer theater" in America, he or she is following in the footsteps of such stars as Gregory Peck, Humphrey Bogart, Robert Montgomery, and Shirley Booth. The theater was founded by entrepreneur Raymond Moore, who thought a professional summer theater close to Boston and the Cape made sense. In the 1920s, theaters would typically close during the summer in the city due to the heat (no air conditioning then!), and people would flock to the seaside. An unknown Bette Davis was an usher in 1928. Every year, the Cape Playhouse holds an open house with self-guided tours through the theater, scene shop, and studio, but the best way to experience the theater is at a live performance.

820 Main St., Dennis, 508-385-3911
capeplayhouse.com

CATCH A FLICK
AT THE WELLFLEET DRIVE-IN

The Wellfleet Drive-In Theatre, in business since 1957, is a Cape Cod mainstay. Generations of fans have made sure that the fun venue stays busy in season from May through September. While the concept may be old, the technology is not. First-run double features play on a 100-by-44-foot screen, with an FM stereo sound system equipped with Dolby Digital sound. For those who prefer air conditioning or go during the off-season, the indoor cinema with four screens is open year-round. In addition to movies, the site is home to the Cape's biggest flea market, where about 200 vendors hawk everything from Cape Cod memorabilia to T-shirts, antiques, jewelry, and other knickknacks. It's a blast to wander around looking for treasures. There's also a playground, a vintage 18-hole miniature golf course, a snack bar, and an outdoor bar and patio.

51 State Hwy., Rte. 6, Wellfleet, 508-349-7176
wellfleetcinemas.com

TAP YOUR TOES
AT THE SOUTH SHORE MUSIC CIRCUS OR CAPE COD MELODY TENT

These sister venues in Cohasset and Hyannis are the only two continuously operated tent theaters-in-the-round in the United States. Owned and operated by the nonprofit South Shore Playhouse Associates, the Music Circus and Melody Tent have a long history dating back decades. Over the years, both venues have attracted major stars of the stage and film, as well as patrons, who love that every seat is within 50 feet of the stage. Among some of the famous names who have performed at one or the other theater are Ginger Rogers, Bob Hope, Debbie Reynolds, Benny Goodman, Dizzy Gillespie, the Beach Boys, the B-52s, Alabama, Pat Benatar, 3 Doors Down, and the list goes on and on. Seeing a favorite band during the summer on the Cape is a special treat, perhaps one worth planning your vacation around.

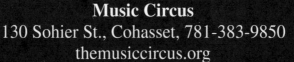

Music Circus
130 Sohier St., Cohasset, 781-383-9850
themusiccircus.org

Melody Tent
21-41 W Main St., Hyannis, 508-775-5630
melodytent.org

CUT LOOSE
AT THE BEACHCOMBER

Oh, this place is so much fun! The restaurant/bar/nightclub, located in a former US Life-Saving Service station at Cahoon Hollow Beach, holds a special place in the hearts of more than one generation of partygoers. The building dates back to 1897 and was one of nine Life-Saving Service stations built on the Outer Cape. Fast forward to 1953, when Russell Gallagher, who had summered in the area as a child, bought it and converted it into a small inn named the Beachcomber. Over the years, it evolved into what it is now. Freshly shucked oysters, boozy frozen mudslides, and awesome live music bring people in by the droves. During the day, it's kid-friendly, with families eating at the restaurant and enjoying the beach. But at night, it's adults-only for music and good times. And you can try to rent the two on-site beach cottages, but they book up fast!

1120 Cahoon Hollow Rd., Wellfleet, 508-349-6055
thebeachcomber.com

SIP VINO
AT TRURO VINEYARDS

This family-owned-and-operated winery was established in 1991, though the property it sits on has been occupied since at least 1813 and even inspired the artist Edward Hopper to paint both the 19th-century Federal house and its barn in 1930. The five-acre farm grows chardonnay, cabernet franc, and merlot grapes, all of which are handpicked at harvest time. Each year, more than a dozen varietals are produced. In addition, the family operates a distillery on the property called South Hollow Spirits, which was the first legal distillery on Cape Cod since Prohibition. To date, the distillery makes rums and gins. Tastings and tours of the vineyard, winery, and distillery are offered at various times, depending on the season. You can also picnic on the grounds if you like, after getting supplies in the well-stocked shop or from a local food truck.

11 Shore Rd., Rte. 6A, North Truro, 508-487-6200
trurovineyardsofcapecod.com

CATCH A SHOW
AT THE POST OFFICE
CAFÉ AND CABARET

With a long and illustrious history, the Post Office Café and Cabaret has served as an important launching pad for many acts in its almost 50 years. In 1974, Phyllis Schlosberg brought the venue into the limelight. She featured Provincetown's now long-reigning drag sensation Varla Jean Merman, as well as camp queen Elvira, Mistress of the Dark. Other famous names to grace its stage include Eartha Kitt, Divine, Carol O'Shaughnessy, Jimmy James, and Thirsty Burlington, among many others. Today you can catch a variety of shows, from drag to burlesque to comedy to live music. Dixie's Lounge, named for a beloved longtime server, is a fun space in the second-floor cabaret room and offers lunch and drinks with great views of Provincetown's pier. Downstairs, there's another bar and a full restaurant.

303 Commercial St., Provincetown, 508-487-0008
postofficecafe.net

ENJOY THE TRADITIONS
AT THE ANNUAL
MV AGRICULTURAL FAIR

The annual Martha's Vineyard Agricultural Society Livestock Show and Fair has been in existence since 1859 and has everything you'd want in a traditional country fair, from racing pigs and tractor pulls to carnival rides and games to delightfully bad-for-you foods like fried dough and corn dogs. My family has been going most summers for more than 20 years, and my daughter even worked at it for a couple of years, opting to earn money taking tickets and picking up trash instead of playing at the beach. The four-day fair is traditionally held the third week of August. Everyone has their favorite events and activities, but I always love heading to the barn to see the prized animals of the hopeful kids and adults who want their rabbit, goat, horse, pig, or even chicken to take home a ribbon.

35 Panhandle Rd., West Tisbury, 508-693-9549
marthasvineyardagriculturalsociety.org

ADVENTURE
WITH ART'S DUNE TOURS

For 75 years, Art's Dune Tours has been taking people through Provincetown's National Seashore for amazing views of the dunes, Pilgrim Lake, and the famous artists' historic dune shacks found there. The dunes are part of the Cape Cod National Seashore, a national park established by President John F. Kennedy in 1961. On a one-hour off-road tour, guides chat about the efforts of conservationists and the National Park Service to stabilize the fragile ecosystem, as well as the draw the region holds for artists of all stripes. It may seem odd to find artist shacks in a national park, but the shacks were there before the park was established. At one point, the shacks were in danger of being demolished, but locals lobbied to protect them, and now they are registered as historic landmarks.

4 Standish St., Provincetown, 508-487-1950
artsdunetours.com

DID YOU KNOW?

To this day, painters, writers, playwrights, and photographers can apply to use the shacks on a short-term basis from the National Park Service, which has agreements with other non-profits that offer artist-in-residence and writer-in-residence programs. Visit nps.gov/caco for more information.

CELEBRATE SUMMER
AT GRAND ILLUMINATION NIGHT

Another island tradition, also held in August, is the lovely Grand Illumination Night in the Martha's Vineyard Camp Meeting Association campground, when inhabitants of the gingerbread houses decorate them with Chinese and Japanese lanterns. This dates all the way back to 1869, when residents wanted to welcome the Massachusetts governor, William Claflin, to the island with a spectacle. At that time, the whole island participated, but since then, it has been limited to the campground. Today, cottage owners go all out with paper lanterns, paper and fabric umbrellas, and similar decor. There's always live music, and, at dusk, the lights are lit all at once, making for a magical scene. It can get really crowded, especially right after dark, but it's delightful to wander around and see the different decorations.

Oak Bluffs, 508-693-0525, ext. 10
mvcma.org/grand-illumination.html

TRY FOR A STRIKE
AT THE BARN

This is the one and only bowling alley on the island, and happily it's a super fun place to hang out. Instead of standard New England candlepin-style bowling, the Barn offers 10 lanes of 10-pin bowling. For the uninformed, the difference is that 10-pin balls are much larger than candlepins, with finger holes, and the pins are cleared away after the first roll. Scoring is automatic, so you don't have to worry about that chore. Besides the bowling alley area, which is decorated with murals of Vineyard towns and photos of US presidents bowling, there's a horseshoe-shaped bar and a dining area. Spectators can watch the action in comfort from tables behind the lanes too. The food is head and shoulders above most bowling alley menus, with dishes like seafood curry, pork schnitzel, and outstanding gourmet pizzas.

13 Uncas Ave., Oak Bluffs, 508-696-9800
thebarnmv.com

ACT LIKE A LOCAL
AT THE RITZ CAFE

If you want to hang out with locals, the Ritz in Oak Bluffs is the place to go. Since 1944, it's served as a hub of island life, with its busy bar, live music, and the spirit of a place "where everybody knows your name." Well, maybe not yours (or mine), but friends shout greetings to one another at all hours over the usually boisterous crowd. It's also one of those rare island spots that stays open year-round. In addition to live music, karaoke and other theme nights also appeal to all crowds. If you want to eat before a show (prior to 8:30 p.m.), you can order Mexican fare from Dilly's Taqueria, which operates out of the Ritz kitchen and offers build-your-own tacos, burritos, quesadillas, and rice bowls.

4 Circuit Ave., Oak Bluffs, 508-693-9851
theritzmv.com

DANCE THE NIGHT AWAY
AT ATLANTIC FISH & CHOPHOUSE

This rather swanky seafood/steakhouse, located right on the harbor in Edgartown, is a great place to dine on dishes like dry-aged ribeye and black truffle lobster mac and cheese (which is to die for), but it has an altogether different scene at night. When dinner service is over, the Atlantic can get quite high-spirited with live music and dancing. If your idea of fun is sipping a drink and watching the boats in the harbor go by, you're in luck with the creative cocktail menu. Try the smoked old-fashioned, which is a dramatic table-side pour, or the Atlantic martini, made with vodka, peach liquor, lime juice, and simple syrup.

2 Main St., Edgartown, 508-627-7001
atlanticmv.com

STAY UP LATE
AT THE GASLIGHT

Besides winning over islanders' hearts with the creative cuisine, this relatively new restaurant and bar, which opened in 2019 in a former theater, gets kudos for its live music offerings at night (usually starting at 10:30 p.m.). Best of all, it's open year-round, which is a bonus for locals who see many venues shut down in the winter. Acts include local, regional, and national bands who perform on an intimate stage with top-of-the-line equipment and state-of-the-art sound systems. Regular local house bands include Foggy Roots, Buckle & Shake, and Coq Au Vin. If you decide to have dinner before a show, the menu features local ingredients with a Japanese twist. Favorites include tuna poke nachos, Japanese curry mussels and fries, and a delicious udon carbonara, which you're probably not going to see on many menus.

3 N Union St., 508-228-6464
gaslightnantucket.com

CATCH A COOL BAND
AT THE CHICKEN BOX

While it may be hard to imagine posh Nantucket having a dive bar, the Chicken Box is probably the closest to it. Opened more than 50 years ago by Willie House, who came to the island from Kentucky and transformed a shack into a Southern fried chicken joint. Over the years, it became more and more popular, and House expanded the venue and eventually brought in live musical acts. It quickly became known as a hot spot for jazz and blues, and even Muddy Waters played there once. Its second owner introduced reggae music to the Chicken Box, and it became a spot where popular reggae bands wanted to play. Along with live music many nights, patrons can play ping pong, shuffleboard, darts, or pool, or just hang out with friends. Simply put, it's a great place to just let loose. And while I haven't been there for the Fourth of July festivities, it's supposed to be a pretty epic night.

16 Dave St., 508-228-9717
thechickenbox.com

STOP AND SMELL THE FLOWERS
AT THE DAFFODIL FESTIVAL

April showers bring . . . the annual Daffodil Festival to Nantucket the last weekend of the month, kicking off spring on the island. For more than 40 years, there has been some version of the popular festival, which was started by the Nantucket Garden Club in 1975. In subsequent years, an antique car parade and a community tailgate picnic were added. In 1978, the club set a goal to plant one million bulbs on the island. Today, it's estimated that there are about two million daffodils blooming there. The festival has grown to include art shows, a pet show, tours, exhibitions, contests, and lectures. There's also the Daffy Hat Contest; a Children's Parade with decorated bikes, strollers, and wagons; and a family picnic at Children's Beach. Fans of the festival tend to go all out, dressing to the nines in elaborate yellow outfits.

daffodilfestival.com

SIP AND SAMPLE
AT THE NANTUCKET
WINE & FOOD FESTIVAL

One mark of spring and of the island gearing up for the summer season is the annual Nantucket Wine & Food Festival in May, which attracts the who's who of the wine and culinary world to the island, as well as other famous faces. More than 3,000 attendees flock to the island's five-day festival for tastings, talks, seminars, cooking contests, classes, parties, lunches, dinners, and galas. Events might include extravagant brunches, live music sessions, and beachside clambakes. It's a good idea to get tickets as soon as they are available because they sell out fast. You can buy individual tickets to whatever might interest you, so you can mix and match, but the opening and closing events and anything with champagne are usually the first to sell out. And you need to book accommodations ASAP too. The festival is based at the White Elephant Resorts, though events are held in various locations on the island.

617-527-9473
nantucketwinefestival.com

SPORTS
AND RECREATION

PLAY
AT SCUSSET BEACH
STATE RESERVATION

Scusset Beach, located on Cape Cod Bay at the east end of the 17.4-mile-long Cape Cod Canal, has a beautiful, sandy beach and a long stone jetty that extends from the end of the service road into the Cape Cod Bay. The main beach is 1.5 miles long, and the reservation offers plenty to do, including swimming, saltwater fishing, picnicking, walking, running, bicycling, bird-watching, ship-watching, and nature programs. In the summer, lifeguards are on duty, and visitors have access to restrooms, showers, and a concession stand. The fish pier area has picnic tables with grills in case you want to cook your catch. You can also access the Cape Cod Canal Bikeway from the beach, and the half-mile trail to the left of the first parking lot leads to Sagamore Hill, where you can visit an area that was once an American Indian meeting ground.

20 Scusset Beach Rd., Sagamore, 508-888-0859
mass.gov/locations/scusset-beach-state-reservation

TIP

Beat high Cape Cod hotel prices by camping! The camping area at the reservation is usually filled to capacity in summer, so book six months in advance to snag one of the 98 RV spots or five tent sites available.

CYCLE
THE CAPE COD RAIL TRAIL

The Cape Cod Rail Trail, a 25-mile paved trail on a former railroad right-of-way, is a delightful way to explore the Cape, passing through six towns, nearby beaches, and other attractions. There are few hills and plenty of space for everyone, including horseback riders, walkers, and runners. The railroad tracks date back to 1848, when the Old Colony Railroad Company ran between Boston and Sandwich. Over time, automobiles replaced the train in popularity, and the service was ended. After years of neglect, the state started converting it into a rail trail. Today, it passes through Dennis, Harwich, Brewster, Orleans, Eastham, and Wellfleet. You can get on the trail from different places, but it makes sense to start from the Salt Pond Visitor Center in Eastham (open year-round), where you can park, pick up maps, and get info about the area. If you don't have your own wheels, there are several places to rent bikes near the trail.

Salt Pond Visitor Center
50 Nauset Rd., Eastham, 508-255-3421
mass.gov/locations/cape-cod-rail-trail

PICK YOUR OWN
AT COONAMESSETT FARM

Coonamessett Farm in Falmouth is so much more than just a place to grab some fresh tomatoes or lettuce at the local farm stand. The 20-acre farm offers an amazing variety of pick-your-own crops (from arugula to zucchini), which are all planted by hand. The farm posts a "What's Ready for Harvesting" sheet and map so you can see what's in season and where to go pick it. In addition, the farm breeds alpacas and is usually home to miniature donkeys, dwarf goats, and chickens, which are all fun to visit. Nonmembers need to purchase a day pass ($8 for ages 2 and up) to visit the farm. Besides produce, the farm sells carved wooden baskets, handmade soaps, alpaca products, jewelry, hand creams, and more.

277 Hatchville Rd., East Falmouth, 508-563-2560
coonamessettfarm.com

PEDAL DOWN
THE SHINING SEA BIKEWAY

Another option for cyclists on the Cape is the Shining Sea Bikeway, an 11-mile bike path that runs from North Falmouth to the Steamship Authority parking lot in Woods Hole. The coastal trail is named after a line from the poem "America the Beautiful," written by Katharine Lee Bates, a Falmouth native. Like the Cape Cod Rail Trail, the path is on a former railroad, which stopped running in 1957. It is mostly an easy, flat route and passes through woodlands, marshes, and salt ponds, as well as the Vineyard Sound. If you have time, you can stop at Trunk River Beach or the Salt Pond Area Bird Sanctuary, a 60-acre preserve.

County Road to Woods Hole, Falmouth
capecodbikeguide.com/shiningsea.asp

TIP

Convenient car parking can be found in two spots. From the Bourne Bridge, head south on Rt. 28 to Falmouth. Turn right onto Locust Road Entry to the bikeway parking area located 1 mile down on the right (just past Pin Oak Way). The North Falmouth parking area is located on the corner of County Road and Route 151.

SPY A SPOUT
WITH HYANNIS
WHALE WATCHER CRUISES

Operating since 1980, Hyannis Whale Watcher Cruises is one of the Cape's oldest whale watch companies. Hopeful whale spotters head out on the comfortable 130-foot Whale Watcher, which offers three viewing levels with plenty of room for passengers to claim their own space at the rail. Inside, there's a full-service snack bar, bathrooms, and lots of seating. On-board naturalists talk about the Cape and marine life as you cruise. And there's plenty to see on the way, including lighthouses and historic dune shacks. Trips are usually about four hours long, leaving from Barnstable Harbor and heading to the Stellwagen Bank National Marine Sanctuary, where whales like to feed on the plentiful fish found there in the warmer months. On the rare occasion when no whales are spotted, passengers are issued a voucher for another trip.

800-287-0374
whales.net

VISIT
THE ISLAND ALPACA COMPANY

There's something so adorable and fun about alpacas, at least to many people, and if you're like me, you'd never pass up an opportunity to see them up close and personal. At the Island Alpaca Company farm, you can see more than 50 of the furry creatures on a self-guided tour. Or you can partake in fun activities such as guided tours, yoga with alpacas, and even alpaca walks. The alpacas are bred for their fleece, and the awesome gift shop is a must-stop for all kinds of gifts, from alpaca sweaters to gloves to toys to yarn. And whenever a new alpaca is born on the farm, the owners hang out a blue or pink flag to let everyone know.

1 Head of the Pond Rd., Oak Bluffs, 508-693-5554
islandalpaca.com

SEE THE DUNES
AT SANDY NECK BEACH PARK

Sandy Neck Beach Park, a six-mile-long barrier beach in Barnstable County, is a beautiful area with a lovely beach, sand dunes, historic dune shacks, maritime forests, freshwater wetland areas, vernal pools, and a salt marsh. Several trails lead to the interior of the park, which you can get to from the beach or from near the gatehouse at the entrance. Conservation is key at the park, and Sandy Neck has been named an Area of Critical Environmental Concern for its fragile dunes and multiple endangered species, including piping plovers and least terns. And it's also been designated a Cultural Historical District because of its dune shacks and cottages (you can see them from the trails), and the Sandy Neck Lighthouse. If you go off the beach, you must always stay on the trails. Check the park's website for nature programs, including guided hikes to look for piping plovers and rare diamondback terrapins (and their nests), as well as talks about local flora and fauna.

425 Sandy Neck Rd., West Barnstable, 508-790-6272
town.barnstable.ma.us/sandyneckpark/default.aspx

TIP

Primitive campers will want to check out the park's remote campsite about three miles away from the parking lot. You couldn't ask for a more exclusive and different beach camping experience if you're willing to hike in (and out) with all your gear. Book well in advance.

MIGRATE
TO MONOMOY NATIONAL WILDLIFE REFUGE

The 7,600-acre Monomoy National Wildlife Refuge, which was established in 1944 to provide habitat to migratory birds, runs from Chatham to Nantucket Sound. The refuge has a lot of bragging rights in terms of wildlife and is a fantastic place for bird-watchers and seal lovers. The expansive property includes Morris, North Monomoy, and South Monomoy Islands and serves as a resting, nesting, and feeding habitat for the federally protected piping plover and several other birds. In addition, South Monomoy Island contains the largest gray seal haul-out site on the US Atlantic Coast. Also of note are the Monomoy Point Light Station and keeper's house on South Monomoy Island, listed on the National Register of Historic Places. The refuge headquarters is on Morris Island, where you'll find a visitor center, beach, and trail system. You can take a guided tour in the summer or explore on your own with self-guided maps.

30 Wikis Way, Chatham, 508-945-0594
fws.gov/refuge/monomoy

TIP

If you don't have your own binoculars, you can borrow a pair at the Visitor Center. You'll want them for better wildlife viewing at the refuge, especially of seals, as you have to stay at least 150 feet away from them.

ENJOY THE OUTDOORS
AT NICKERSON STATE PARK

Located in Brewster, this approximately 1,900-acre state park is a veritable playground for outdoors lovers, with eight freshwater ponds for swimming, boating, and fishing; miles of trails for hiking; paved trails that lead to the Cape Cod Rail Trail for cyclists; and more than 400 campsites for overnighters. Birders also flock here to see everything from woodpeckers to ospreys. The park is named after the Nickerson family. Samuel Nickerson, a Chatham native, founded the First National Bank of Chicago. His son, Roland C. Nickerson, and Roland's wife, Addie, had an estate here. Addie donated the land to the state in 1934. The Friends of Nickerson State Park offer special programs in the summer, such as animal ambassador encounters and guided bike rides.

3488 Main St., Brewster, 508-896-3491
mass.gov/locations/nickerson-state-park

CAPER
AT THE CAPE COD NATIONAL SEASHORE

Composed of 44,600 acres, running from Chatham to Provincetown with 40 miles of coastline, the Cape Cod National Seashore is the most singular attraction of the Cape. It was protected as a national park by President John F. Kennedy in 1961, and there are numerous beaches, marshes, ponds, forests, cranberry bogs, and historical sites to explore. Activities include hiking, biking, swimming, fishing, skating, surfing, boating, visiting lighthouses, and enjoying ranger-led talks and guided tours. Begin your visit at the Salt Pond Visitor Center in Eastham, where you can learn about the area's history before heading to any number of spots in the park. Pick up maps, talk to helpful rangers, get an overview of the park, watch an orientation movie, and visit the bookstore and the small museum.

50 Nauset Rd., Eastham, 508-255-3421
nps.gov/caco

GO BIRD-WATCHING
AT WELLFLEET BAY
WILDLIFE SANCTUARY

This 1,100-acre Mass Audubon sanctuary on Cape Cod is a magnet for wildlife with its salt marsh, sandy beach, pine woods, freshwater pond, and rare heath land. An amazing 260-plus species of birds have been recorded at the sanctuary, so chances are pretty good you'll encounter some on your visit. There are six trails to explore, including Goose Pond Trail, which goes through pine and oak woodlands, past two ponds, along a coastal heath, and around the edges of a salt marsh. To get to the beach, take the Boardwalk Trail across the salt marsh to see what's going on at the tidal flats. Inside the LEED Platinum-certified Nature Center, you can learn about the award-winning building and its green design on a self-guided tour.

291 State Hwy., Rte. 6, South Wellfleet, 508-349-2615
massaudubon.org/get-outdoors/wildlife-sanctuaries/wellfleet-bay

TIP

For decades, the sanctuary has offered two-to-three-day field courses for adults who want a deeper dive into an environmental topic unique to the area. Options have included Coastal Birding for Beginners, Ecology by Kayak, and Sea Turtle & Marine Animal Strandings, among others. Check the website for information.

SURF THE WAVES
AT KATAMA/SOUTH BEACH

Hands down, one of the most popular beaches on the island is Katama, or South Beach, a three-mile barrier beach facing the Atlantic Ocean on the southern (Katama) area of Edgartown. Body surfers and those who like to swim in big waves love this beach, but those with families can also enjoy it because of the calm salt pond on the other side. You can spend the entire day going back and forth to experience both, something I've done countless times with my family. Another perk of this beach is the plentiful and free parking, which means you can almost always find a spot (this can't be said for all MV beaches).

555 Katama Rd., Edgartown
mvy.com/beaches.html

TAKE A HIKE
AT FELIX NECK WILDLIFE SANCTUARY

A Mass Audubon property, Felix Neck Wildlife Sanctuary offers about four miles of trails on the 200-acre preserve, which includes woodlands, meadows, ponds, salt marshes, and shores. Each of its four trails is about a half-mile in length, perfect for anyone with small children looking for a short walk in nature. The Sassafras to Shad (Yellow) Trail leads to a footbridge over Turtle Pond, where you might spy frogs and turtles. The Marsh (Red) Trail offers views of State Beach. The Jessica Hancock Memorial (Green) Trail goes through a freshwater bog, and the Old Farm Road (Blue) Trail leads to Sengekontacket Pond. You can, of course, combine the trails for a longer jaunt. There's also a nature center, and guides lead a variety of themed hikes and tours, including stargazing, spotting snakes, bird-watching, and kayaking.

100 Felix Neck Dr., Edgartown, 508-627-4850
massaudubon.org/get-outdoors/wildlife-sanctuaries/felix-neck

ADMIRE
THE AQUINNAH CLIFFS

The Aquinnah Cliffs (once called Gay Head) are located on the western point of the island and are part of the 485-acre Wampanoag reservation. Composed of red clay, the cliffs are a striking and beautiful natural attraction, but they are in danger of erosion. In fact, the historic Gay Head Light had to be moved back from the edge of the cliffs in an epic operation in 2015. You can walk along the lower beach paths to see the cliffs from below or enjoy the views from up top from the lighthouse (in season) or from an extensive overlook platform. Near the lighthouse, you'll find several Wampanoag shops and snack bars, plus the Aquinnah Wampanoag Indian Museum, most of which are open seasonally (generally late May through early October).

31 Aquinnah Cir., Aquinnah
mvy.com/aquinnah.html

TIP

To see a cool timelapse video of the lighthouse being moved, visit gayheadlight.org.

SWIM
AT JOSEPH SYLVIA STATE BEACH

This two-mile-long barrier beach, which separates Sengekontacket Pond from Nantucket Sound, is quite popular with families, as the waves are generally small, and it's easy to cross the street to swim in the pond if it's too windy or the ocean water is too cold. Part of it is also referred to as the "Bend-in-the-Road" beach, for obvious reasons. There are lifeguards on duty in season and a place to rent kayaks. This beach is also home to the so-called Jaws bridge, made famous in the iconic film, and where today brave souls—or foolhardy ones, depending on your point of view—jump off into the water below.

Beach Rd., Oak Bluffs/Edgartown, 508-696-3840
dukescounty.org/natural-resources/pages/marthas-vineyard-beaches

DID YOU KNOW?

Close to Oak Bluffs is Inkwell Beach, famous for its popularity with Black residents and visitors. As early as the 19th century, the Vineyard, especially Oak Bluffs, was a popular summer resort community for African Americans. The name "Inkwell" was used as a slur by whites to refer to the beach. In time, that pejorative was flipped on its head and is now used with pride by its beachgoers.

GANDER THROUGH
POLLY HILL ARBORETUM

No matter the season, the Polly Hill Arboretum offers something to see and is a lovely place to explore, with stone walls, meadows, and fields, plus rare trees and shrubs from around the world. Highlights include North Tisbury azaleas, camellias, hollies, conifers, rhododendrons, crab apples, and magnolias, among others. The kousa dogwood allée and the monkey puzzle tree are popular stops. The arboretum is named after its founder, Polly Hill, an avid horticulturist who passed away at age 100 in 2007 after experimenting with plants for 50 years. The 70-acre property was established in 1998 as a nonprofit, ensuring that her legacy lives on. Programs such as tours, lectures, workshops, and even plant sales are often offered.

809 State Rd., West Tisbury, 508-693-9426
pollyhillarboretum.org

WATCH THE SUNSET
AT MENEMSHA BEACH

This small beach is one of the best places to catch the sunset on the island. It's located in Chilmark, in what can only be referred to as a charming working fishing village, and you'll find some shops and a few places to eat, including the best spot in New England for a lobster roll, along with the beach. Bring a blanket, your beverage of choice, a picnic (or get a lobster roll from Larsen's Fish Market), and whatever else you might need, and get there early enough in the afternoon so you can snag a parking space in the small lot. You can thank me later.

56 Basin Rd., Menemsha, Chilmark

GO OFF-ROADING
ON CHAPPY

Just off the coast of the island in Edgartown is the tiny island of Chappaquiddick, a delightful place to get away from it all, especially if you get an over-sand vehicle permit to explore. It's fun to drive on the beach and find your own secluded spot of sand to soak in the sun. On the island, there's the Cape Poge Wildlife Refuge and Mytoi Japanese-style garden (both Trustees properties). If you don't have a lot of time, it's still worth the very, very short ferry ride to the island and back for the novelty. The journey is just 527 feet! Both Chappy and the ferry have some notoriety: the island is still known as the place where Senator Ted Kennedy and Mary Jo Kopechne had a car accident in 1969, resulting in her death; the ferry was used in the film *Jaws*.

53 Dock St., Edgartown
chappyferry.com/chappaquiddick/explore-chappaquiddick

DID YOU KNOW?

The Trustees of Reservations, founded by landscape architect Charles Eliot in 1891, is the country's first (and Massachusetts') largest preservation and conservation nonprofit. The Trustees cares for more than 100 special places around Massachusetts, including four places in this book, and offers more than 5,000 programs and events year-round. For more information, visit thetrustees.org.

GET REMOTE
AT CAPE POGE WILDLIFE REFUGE

This 516-acre wildlife sanctuary, a Trustees property, is located on Chappaquiddick, so some planning is required if you want to go overland in an allowed vehicle (along 14 miles of trails) or take a guided tour. Gorgeous beaches with nary a person around offer a stunning setting, and quite a few anglers like to fish here. The property is also a protected nesting area for a variety of New England shorebirds, so keep a sharp eye out for them. Trustees naturalists lead jeep tours to the Cape Poge Lighthouse, as well as kayak and seaside tours in season.

Dike Rd., Chappaquiddick, 508-627-7689
thetrustees.org/place/cape-poge-wildlife-refuge

FUN FACT
The Cape Poge light flashing 63 feet above the dune sand can be seen by sailors nine miles out to sea.

MEANDER
THROUGH MYTOI

Yet another Trustees property, Mytoi is a completely unexpected and magical place to visit. Created in the 1950s by a local resident and gifted to the nonprofit in the 1970s, the Japanese-style garden feels like a secret you've been let in on. Once you walk through the gates, you truly feel like you aren't on the Vineyard at all. Meandering paths pass through birch trees, camellias, and a stone garden; over a footbridge; and by a hillside garden. Look for turtles, frogs, and goldfish in the pond covered by lily pads, or just sit on a beach and relax. Plants include both native and exotic species. If you are looking for a place to unwind and commune with nature, this is it.

Dike Rd., Chappaquiddick, 508-627-7689
thetrustees.org/place/mytoi

MAKE A BEELINE
TO THE BEACHES

Although Nantucket is small, it has plenty of beachfront to enjoy. If for some reason you don't like a particular beach, well, just head to the next! The most popular are Brant Point (close to town, scenic, with a strong current and no lifeguard), Jetties (a bike or bus ride from town, with lifeguards, concessions, and a bathhouse), Children's (an easy walk from town with a playground), and Surfside (on the south shore, popular with families and kite surfers alike). There are plenty of others, all with their own charms, and everyone has their favorite. It's fun to figure out which one might be yours.

nantucket.net/beaches

WATCH FOR WHALES
WITH SHEARWATER EXCURSIONS

Shearwater offers plenty of tours, but its whale-watching excursion is the flagship trip. The six-hour adventure on a 47-foot catamaran leaves from the Town Pier. You'll head out to look for humpback, finback, and minke whales, accompanied by a naturalist who will talk about the island, whales, and wildlife. The family-owned-and-operated business started in 1999 and is named for owner Captain Blair Perkins's favorite bird, the shearwater. Another whale-focused excursion is the Whaling History Tour, where you'll see landmarks from the Nantucket whaling era and learn about life aboard the whaleship *Essex*, featured in the film *In the Heart of the Sea* by Nantucket author Nathaniel Philbrick.

Straight Wharf, 508-228-7037
shearwaterexcursions.com

BIKE AROUND
NANTUCKET

Considering Nantucket's tiny size, just 14 miles long by 3.5 miles wide, the island is an ideal place to cycle. There are more than 33 miles of bike paths for you to explore, and if you don't bring your own bicycle, you can easily rent one. Many hotels also offer bikes as a guest amenity. Most of Nantucket's bike paths are for pedestrians and cyclists, and they are usually separate from and adjacent to the roads, so you don't have to worry about cars. Some of the more popular routes include the Cliff Road Path, running from Cliff Beach to Madaket Road; 5.7-mile Madaket Road Path, which begins at Caton Circle and leads to Madaket Beach; and Surfside Road Path, a 2.2-mile path leading from the high school to Surfside Beach. You can pick up a map at bike shops or download one from the Nantucket town website.

nantucket-ma.gov/985/bike-paths

SET SAIL
ON THE *ENDEAVOR*

I'm not sure how many opportunities there are to set sail with the person who built the boat you're going to sail aboard, but on Nantucket—if you go out with Captain James Genthner on the *Endeavor*, a Coast Guard–certified vessel—you can. This is the longest operating sailboat charter on Nantucket, and Captain Jim offers both public and private trips around the island. If you want to, you can help the crew set sail, or you can bring a picnic and simply relax. From Nantucket's maritime history to traditional boat building, Captain Jim is a wealth of knowledge. Book well in advance for this special experience.

Straight Wharf, 508-228-5585
endeavorsailing.com

CULTURE AND HISTORY

CHECK OUT
THE CAPE COD CANAL VISITOR CENTER

This 17.5-mile waterway serves as the gateway to the Cape and is operated and maintained by the US Army Corps of Engineers, New England District. It's one of the Corps' busiest projects, with tens of thousands of vessels using the waterway every year. You can learn all about the history of the canal at the Cape Cod Canal Visitor Center, which gives a great overview. Activities include scanning live radar to locate vessels in the waterway, "captaining" a virtual boat through the canal, and watching films about the wildflowers and wildlife in and along the canal. You can also board a retired 40-foot patrol boat. The center is staffed by the US Army Corps of Engineers Park Rangers and volunteers, who are happy to chat about the canal.

60 Ed Moffitt Dr., Sandwich, 508-833-9678
nae.usace.army.mil/missions/recreation/cape-cod-canal

BE DAZZLED
AT THE SANDWICH GLASS MUSEUM

This surprisingly interactive museum offers more to see and do than you might expect, from a 20-minute video detailing the creation of the Boston & Sandwich Glass Company to fascinating demos. Settled in 1637 and incorporated in 1639, Sandwich is the oldest town on Cape Cod, and its glass factory played a big role in the American glass industry. The fascinating and fun Levine Lighting Gallery, which is dark when you enter, showcases 50 Sandwich lighting devices dating from 1825 to the electric light bulb. One by one, the lamps light up, giving you a visual timeline of progress in lighting technology. Don't miss the glass-blowing demo, where you'll watch molten glass, drawn from the furnace, being blown and pressed into exquisite shapes. Stop in the shop to pick up beautiful and unusual souvenirs.

129 Main St., Sandwich, 508-888-0251
sandwichglassmuseum.org

WANDER AROUND
THE HERITAGE MUSEUMS & GARDENS

This 100-acre property, founded in 1969, is the largest public garden in southern New England. The varieties of trees, shrubs, and flowers number in the thousands. Highlights include a charming windmill, which was built in Orleans, Massachusetts, in 1800; a working vintage 1912 carousel; a labyrinth; and Hidden Hollow, a magical two-acre playground for children. There's also a collection of classic cars, American decorative and folk art, and traveling exhibits spread out over three buildings. In May and June, the impressive collection of rhododendrons, numbering in the thousands, is generally in bloom and not to be missed. I especially like going off the main path to explore the several miles of nature trails, which you'll often have all to yourself.

67 Grove St., Sandwich, 508-888-3300
heritagemuseumsandgardens.org

TIP
In late November and December, the entire property is transformed into a winter wonderland, with light displays, hands-on activities, music, and more. Get tickets early, as this always sells out.

EXPLORE A QUIRKY MIND
AT THE EDWARD GOREY HOUSE

Once the home of the world-renowned artist Edward Gorey, this 200-year-old former sea captain's house (which Gorey bought in 1979) is now a museum dedicated to Gorey's life, his work, and his love of animals. He is perhaps best known for *The Gashlycrumb Tinies*, his iconic, macabre, and hysterical alphabet book announcing the demise of 26 very unfortunate children, or his delightful animated sequences on PBS's *Mystery!* There is no mistaking Gorey's signature touch. Stiff Victorians, sinister Edwardians, doomed infants, odd creatures, and mysterious landscapes are classic Gorey, but he was also a playwright and a set and costume designer. Gorey was also an avid collector of random stuff, including figurines, cheese graters, potato mashers, skulls, spheres, stone frogs, ticket stubs, and tarot decks, among other items, which you might see on display.

8 Strawberry Ln., Yarmouth Port, 508-362-3909
edwardgoreyhouse.org

TIP

Every year, the museum offers wall calendars featuring different Gorey works (he was quite prolific!), which sell out very quickly. They are a fun gift to give or receive and since they change every year, you never know what you'll get. Check the museum's website in the summer for the following year's calendar.

DIVE INTO
THE WOODS HOLE SCIENCE AQUARIUM

The country's oldest marine aquarium, established in 1885, is home to about 140 species of marine animals found in the Northeast and Middle Atlantic waters. You can expect to see a variety of creatures, such as cod fish, horseshoe crabs, and sea urchins. Dedicated to educating the public, the aquarium allows visitors behind the scenes, where you can see the staff feed animals, clean tanks, and work on the life-support systems. In addition to providing a home for stranded seals, staff also rehabilitate and release cold-stunned turtles who are sometimes found stranded. The cool "Sounds of the Sea" exhibit gives insight into what marine life sounds like in the oceans. In the summer, naturalists often lead tours on local beaches. It's a fantastic and fun way to learn about the animals found in the Cape waters.

166 Water St., Woods Hole, 508-495-2001
fisheries.noaa.gov/new-england-mid-atlantic/outreach-and-education/
woods-hole-science-aquarium

TRACE A LEGACY
ON THE JFK TRAIL

Located in Hyannis, where Rose Fitzgerald Kennedy and Joseph P. Kennedy Sr. purchased a summer home in 1928, the 1.6-mile Kennedy Legacy Trail covers 10 sites significant to the powerful political family. While it was designed as a self-guided walking tour, if you can't make the trip or the weather doesn't cooperate, the trail's excellent website details each site with text and videos. If you do walk the trail, you can listen to audio descriptions on your mobile phone. The trail begins at the John F. Kennedy Hyannis Museum, and highlights include St. Francis Xavier Church, the summer parish for most of the Kennedy family; the Hyannis Armory, where John F. Kennedy accepted winning the 35th presidential election; and other sites where important events occurred, such as when President Kennedy signed legislation in 1961 to establish the Cape Cod National Seashore.

397 Main St., Hyannis, 508-790-3077
kennedylegacytrail.com

GO LOCAL
AT THE CAPE COD MUSEUM OF ART

Located on the grounds of the Cape Playhouse, this museum features a permanent collection of more than 850 works by notable Cape Cod–associated artists, including Charles Hawthorne, who founded America's first artists' colony in 1899 in Provincetown. The museum's mission is to be a home for Cape-related artwork, so both locals and visitors can enjoy art from the region, which has served as inspiration to so many. Outside the museum, you'll find a lovely sculpture garden to explore, while inside there are seven galleries. Among the collection highlights are a print by Alexander Calder; works by plen air painter John Joseph Enneking; and a painting by Hans Hofmann, a renowned Provincetown artist and teacher who is considered by many to be the father of abstract expressionism. In addition to permanent works, the museum offers temporary exhibitions, special events, workshops, and classes.

60 Hope Ln., Dennis, 508-385-4477
ccmoa.org

HOP OVER
TO THE TOAD HALL
CLASSIC SPORTS CAR MUSEUM

There probably aren't many places, if any, where you can see more than 50 red classic sports cars all in the same place. The only one I know of is in Hyannis Port, where you can visit Bill Putman, "innkeeper of sorts," at the Simmons Homestead Inn. Putman, who turned a historic 19th-century captain's house into a bed and breakfast in 1988, started with just a few sports cars, but his private collection grew and grew. When he had more than three dozen, he decided to open the collection to the public. The unifying theme is that all the cars are red, which explains the museum's name, Toad Hall. In the classic 1908 book *The Wind in the Willows* by Kenneth Grahame, the leading character is Toad, lord of Toad Hall, who is obsessed with motorcars, and—you guessed it—they are all red.

288 Scudder Ave., Hyannis Port, 508-778-4934
toadhallcars.com

BE INSPIRED
AT THE NANTUCKET
SHIPWRECK & LIFESAVING MUSEUM

This museum features permanent and changing exhibits detailing the history of Nantucket lifesaving efforts over the years, including details about famous shipwrecks and rescues, equipment, and how the Coast Guard works today. In the 19th century, hundreds of ships passed by Nantucket daily, facing treacherous conditions, which resulted in more than 700 shipwrecks. Islanders did what they could to rescue survivors and recover bodies. It was a grueling and dangerous volunteer job. There are about 5,000 artifacts and items in the collection, ranging from vintage photos to a Fresnel lens to beach carts once used in rescues.

158 Polpis Rd., Nantucket, 508-228-1885
eganmaritime.org/shipwreck-lifesaving-museum

DID YOU KNOW?

Much of the permanent collection in the
museum comes from Robert Caldwell, a
Nantucket man who served in the Coast Guard
in World War II and became fascinated by the
Coast Guard's roots on Nantucket.

EXPLORE MORE
AT THE CAPE COD
MUSEUM OF NATURAL HISTORY

There's a lot to discover at this museum, which was founded in 1954 to advance and share knowledge of the Cape's natural environment. There are two floors of exhibits, covering everything from whales to birds to live marine science. You'll also find an ever-changing aquarium with different species of crustaceans, fish, mollusks, frogs, turtles, and snakes. Another exhibit, "People of the Land: The Wampanoag," which was created with local Wampanoag people and Plimoth Plantation, looks at the original inhabitants of the region and displays archaeological artifacts. The museum sits on 80 acres, adjacent to 300 acres of town-owned conservation land, with three nature trails that go through woodlands, salt marsh, and the shore of Cape Cod Bay, plus a wildflower garden. The 1.3-mile John Wing Trail is the most popular; it ends at a barrier beach and the tidal pools of the bay.

869 Main St., Rte. 6A, Brewster, 508-896-3867
ccmnh.org

LEARN ISLAND LORE
AT THE MARTHA'S VINEYARD MUSEUM

The Martha's Vineyard Museum, situated on one acre overlooking the Lagoon Pond and outer Vineyard Haven harbor, is the best place to get an overview of the island's rich history. It has more than 15,000 objects in its collection, from maritime items to archaeological materials. Exhibits include "One Island, Many Stories," which explores the history of the island. The "Challenge of the Sea" exhibit is an overview of island shipwrecks, navigation, lifesaving, and weather. Artifacts from those shipwrecks, such as from the steamer *City of Columbus*, which wrecked in 1883, are fascinating time capsules. "Flashes of Brilliance" tells the history of island lighthouses, with an 1854 Fresnel lens from the Gay Head Light hanging in the two-story glass pavilion. Don't skip Doherty Hall, located behind the museum, which houses large items such as whaling and fishing vessels.

151 Lagoon Pond Rd., Vineyard Haven, 508-627-4441
mvmuseum.org

TAKE IN
THE TOWERING PILGRIM MONUMENT AND PROVINCETOWN MUSEUM

There's no missing the 252-foot-tall granite Pilgrim Monument in Provincetown, which can be seen from everywhere in this fun beach town. The monument was modeled after the Torre del Mangia in Siena, Italy, and is the tallest all-granite structure in the United States. President Theodore Roosevelt commissioned it in 1907 to commemorate the site of the Mayflower Pilgrims' first landing in the New World in 1620. In 1910, President William Howard Taft dedicated the finished tower. Today, you can climb to the top for amazing views, but it's about a 10-minute hike, with 116 steps and 60 ramps. The Provincetown Museum, next to the monument, features exhibits covering the arrival of the Pilgrims, the town's maritime history, the construction of the monument, and re-creations of a 19th-century sea captain's parlor at home and his quarters at sea.

1 High Pole Hill Rd., Provincetown, 508-487-1310
pilgrim-monument.org

FUN FACT

The tower's architect, Willard Thomas Sears, a prominent architect in the late 19th and early 20th centuries, also designed Old South Church, the Isabella Stewart Gardner Museum, and the Cyclorama in Boston, as well as Campobello Park in New Brunswick, Canada.

LIGHTHOUSE-HOP
ON MARTHA'S VINEYARD

There are five lighthouses on the island: East Chop, Edgartown, Gay Head, Cape Poge, and West Chop. The island's location has historically been tricky for ships, with one tide coming in from Boston, affecting the south side of the island, and another coming from Rhode Island, affecting the north. Reefs, rocks, and shoals are everywhere, adding another level of challenge for ships. The aptly named Devil's Bridge off Aquinnah wrecked the steamship *City of Columbus* on January 18, 1884, costing 120 crew and passengers their lives. Different entities are in charge of the various lighthouses, so access and tours vary quite a bit; West Chop, which is privately owned, is not open to the public. But whether or not you can climb up the lighthouses, maybe they are best enjoyed from afar anyway.

FUN FACT

In 2015, the 400-ton Gay Head Lighthouse was successfully moved, with no damage, 129 feet away from the eroding cliffs, buying what experts think is at least another 150 years of safety before erosion may require another move.

VINEYARD LIGHTHOUSES

East Chop
229 E Chop Ave., Oak Bluffs, 508-627-4441
mvmuseum.org/visit/east-chop

Edgartown
121 N Water St., Edgartown, 508-627-4441
mvmuseum.org/visit/edgartown

Gay Head
Aquinnah Cir., Aquinnah, 508-645-2300
gayheadlight.org

Cape Poge
Dike Rd., Chappaquiddick, 508-627-3599
thetrustees.org

West Chop
Main St., Tisbury
nps.gov/Nr/travel/maritime/wes.htm

VISIT
THE OLD WHALING CHURCH

This 1843 building, designed by Frederick Baylies Jr., was built by local shipwrights for Edgartown's wealthy Methodist whaling captains and their families in the booming days of whaling. It's considered one of the best examples of Greek Revival architecture in New England and is quite the showstopper. Outside, it looks like an ancient temple, with six Doric columns, and it's crowned with a Gothic Revival clock tower. The interior has a curved ceiling supported by complex trusses ingeniously constructed out of massive timbers. Murals inside depict unfurled leaves, curved vines, and stylized rosettes. And the rear wall boasts a full-scale trompe l'oeil mural that deceives viewers' eyes into thinking that a carved arch leads to a light-filled room beyond. Today the property is owned and managed by the nonprofit Vineyard Trust and used for community events, special celebrations, and performances.

89 Main St., Edgartown, 508-627-4440
vineyardtrust.org/property/old-whaling-church

SNAG THE BRASS RING
ON THE FLYING HORSES CAROUSEL

No matter your age, attempting to grab the brass ring as your horse goes around on the carousel is a hoot. For sure, this activity is probably best for the kids, but even watching and cheering them on at the oldest operating platform carousel in the country is a blast. Built in 1876 and originally launched on Coney Island, the Flying Horses Carousel has been carefully preserved, with its hand-painted horses with glass eyes and horsehair manes. It's been on the island since 1884 and is owned by the nonprofit Vineyard Trust. The brass ring challenge is to collect as many rings as you can as you ride by a metal ring dispenser (one within reach of the outside row and one within reach of the inside row) to try to get the coveted brass ring—and win a free ride.

33 Lake Ave., Oak Bluffs, 508-627-4440
vineyardtrust.org/property/flying-horses-carousel

WANDER
THE MV CAMP MEETING ASSOCIATION GROUNDS

One of the most unique places on the Vineyard is located in Oak Bluffs. About 300 tiny "gingerbread" houses that look like elaborate playhouses for children were originally built by 19th-century Methodists who came to the Vineyard in the summer to worship. The idea of holding camp meetings for religious purposes was introduced by the Presbyterians, with Baptists and Methodists taking part in Kentucky prior to 1820. New England Methodists soon followed suit. Their original temporary canvas tents soon came to be replaced by permanent, colorfully painted cottages. Today these are strictly seasonal and are either privately owned by camping descendants (some who do rent them out) or members of the Camp Meeting Association. Free concerts, guest speakers, and movie nights are held at the Tabernacle complex in the middle of the campground and are open to the public. Walking tours of the grounds are offered in the summer.

80 Trinity Park, Oak Bluffs, 508-693-0525
mvcma.org

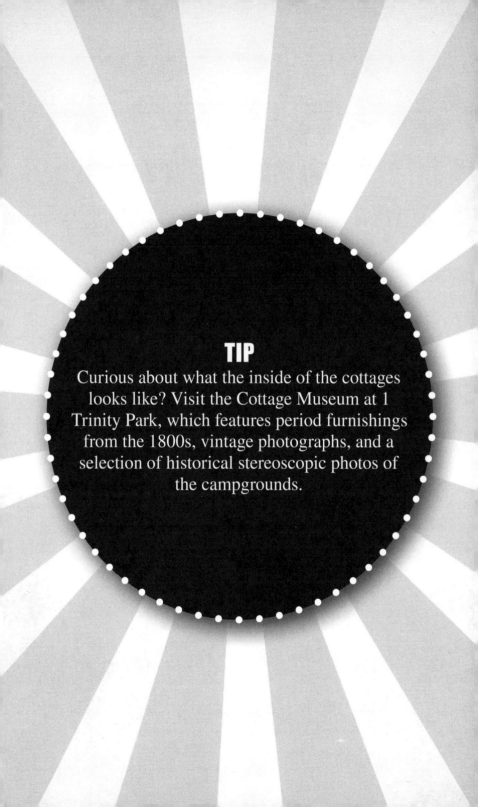

TIP
Curious about what the inside of the cottages looks like? Visit the Cottage Museum at 1 Trinity Park, which features period furnishings from the 1800s, vintage photographs, and a selection of historical stereoscopic photos of the campgrounds.

GO INDIE
AT THE MV FILM SOCIETY

The nonprofit Martha's Vineyard Film Society, which opened in 2012 with a 176-seat theater in Vineyard Haven, screens independent films, classics, documentaries, and world cinema and also hosts film-related speakers and filmmakers, educational programs, and other special events. In a typical year, the society shows more than 200 feature and short films and schedules 1,000 different programs, offering something for every kind of film fan. The organization also produces the annual Martha's Vineyard International Film Festival, the MV Environmental Film Festival, the FILMUSIC Festival, the SPECTRUM Film Festival (focused on LBGTQ+ issues and films), MV Documentary Week, and the Women in Film Festival. It's a great venue, and there's not a bad seat in the house.

79 Beach Rd., Vineyard Haven, 508-696-9369
mvfilmsociety.com

SAIL
TO THE WHALING MUSEUM

The Whaling Museum is a great place to get an overview of the importance of whaling to Nantucket and the island's history over the past 400 years. In nine galleries, you'll find permanent and rotating exhibits covering everything from fossils to decorative arts. Among the most striking exhibits is a 46-foot sperm whale skeleton that washed ashore in 1998, an 1849 Fresnel lens from the old Sankaty Head Lighthouse, and a restored 1847 candle factory. The stunning collection of scrimshaw art is considered among the best in the world. Whalers at sea would create elaborately engraved or carved pieces out of spare whale bones and teeth to pass the time, and there are spectacular specimens here, including boxes, canes, tools, and more.

15 Broad St., Nantucket, 508-228-1894
nha.org/visit/museums-and-tours/whaling-museum

DID YOU KNOW?

The Whaleship *Essex*, which sailed from Nantucket in 1819 and was famously rammed by a whale in 1820, was the inspiration for Herman Melville's *Moby-Dick*. The museum has excellent exhibits on its history.

● ●

VISIT THE MUSEUM
OF AFRICAN AMERICAN HISTORY

This museum is composed of two historic sites—the African Meeting House and the Florence Higginbotham House—that were at the center of the thriving 19th-century African American community on Nantucket. The Meeting House is the only public building constructed and occupied by African Americans in the 19th century left on the island. The Seneca Boston-Florence Higginbotham House, built before the Revolutionary War, was purchased in 1774 by Seneca Boston. He was a weaver and formerly enslaved man whose family maintained the house until 1918. The Black Heritage Trail in Nantucket features nine stops and is divided into two segments, Downtown and New Guinea. Stops include the Whaling Museum (to see the portrait of Nantucket's only known Black whaling captain, Absalom Boston), the Unitarian Church (where Frederick Douglass and Booker T. Washington both spoke), and Anna Gardner's House (she helped to convene the island's first Anti-Slavery Convention in 1841).

29 York St., Nantucket, 508-228-9833
maah.org

GET TO THE POINT
AT THE COSKATA-COATUE WILDLIFE REFUGE AND GREAT POINT LIGHT

Great Point Light, officially named Nantucket Light, is on the northernmost point of the island at the Coskata-Coatue Wildlife Refuge. With about 1,100 acres, Coskata-Coatue is composed of a pair of long peninsulas, with more than 200 acres of maritime dunes, a red cedar savannah and woodland, and a mature maritime oak forest. If you really want to get away from it all, this is a great place to visit. Seals are often spotted here snacking on fish they catch in the riptide. Visitors can hike along the Beach Trail, Inside Trail, or Coskata Woods Trail or take a tour of the Great Point Light with the Trustees (in season). The lighthouse was built in 1784 as a wooden tower. It was destroyed by fire in 1816 and rebuilt the following year as a stone structure. That lasted until 1984, when it was destroyed by a bad storm and rebuilt yet again.

Wauwinet Rd., Nantucket, 508-228-5646
thetrustees.org/place/coskata-coatue-wildlife-refuge

NOSE AROUND
THE NANTUCKET ATHENEUM

The Nantucket Atheneum, which is actually the island's library, is located in a Greek Revival–style building listed on the National Register of Historic Places. Inside, artworks and artifacts detail the island's history. The Atheneum dates back to the early 1800s, when the Nantucket Mechanics Social Library and the Columbian Library Society joined forces. In 1833, the library moved to the renovated Universalist Church. The following year, it was incorporated as the Nantucket Atheneum. The Great Fire of 1846 destroyed the original building and virtually all its collections, but it was rebuilt in 1847 and became a free public library in 1900.

1 India St., Nantucket, 508-228-1110
nantucketatheneum.org

FUN FACTS

Atheneum cofounder Charles G. Coffin, a wealthy businessman who owned a fleet of whaling ships, offered a lending library on all his ships. David Joy, the other cofounder, invented a process for the manufacture of spermaceti candles. A fervent abolitionist, he introduced Frederick Douglass as a speaker at the Atheneum during the antislavery convention of 1841. Finally, 18-year-old Maria Mitchell was the first librarian of the Atheneum, working there for 20 years. She discovered a comet and became the first professor of astronomy at Vassar College and the first woman elected to the American Academy of Arts and Sciences.

SHOPPING AND FASHION

CRAWL
THE CAPE & ISLANDS
BOOKSTORE TRAIL

There are trails for everyone from beer drinkers to oyster fans, so why not one for book lovers? I could have included all the bookstores in the region in this book, but this isn't a book about books! But here's the next best thing: the Cape & Islands Bookstore Trail. Created a couple of years ago by local independent bookstore owners, the trail includes more than 20 shops. You can visit the group's website to see the list, click links to the individual stores, and download a map. So far, the participating shops include one on Martha's Vineyard, two on Nantucket, and others spread out across the Cape.

capeandislandsbookstoretrail.com

BROWSE
THE BREWSTER STORE

Straight out of central casting, this shop, located in an 1852 church turned general store in 1866, has been a hub of the community since it opened. From candies to antiques and everything in between, it's the type of place where it's impossible to leave without buying something. The benches out front are popular with locals and visitors alike to sit and enjoy a cup of coffee or an ice cream from the adjacent Brewster Scoop. Whether you need a sweatshirt for chilly nights, a kitchen tool for your summer rental, a postcard for faraway friends, a souvenir to take home, a book to read on the beach, toys for the kids, or just a snack, this is the spot to find it.

1935 Main St., Brewster, 508-896-3744
brewsterstore.com

TREASURE HUNT
AT BUZZARDS BAY ANTIQUES

With 15 dealers who specialize in different types of antiques, collectibles, or vintage items spread out over 7,000 square feet, you are sure to find something that speaks to you at this sprawling space. The dealers are constantly changing up their inventory, so every time you visit, something new awaits. If you do see something you like, grab it right away—it probably won't be there the next time you stop in. Among the various collections, you'll find antiques, glassware, handmade jewelry, vintage toys, furniture, games, silverware, and all sorts of treasures. You can easily spend a couple of hours exploring every corner here, a perfect activity for a rainy day (though you shouldn't wait for bad weather to go shopping!).

61 Main St., Buzzards Bay, 774-302-4065
buzzardsbayantique.com

BOOK IT
TO TITCOMB'S BOOKSHOP

The backstory of this bookstore is as charming as the bookstore itself. In the 1960s, the Titcomb children discovered a collection of rare papers and books, dating back to the 1600s, in a barn on their new property in Connecticut. This led to a mail-order catalog business. The children got a Saint Bernard puppy with the proceeds of the first sale, and, over the years, the business grew and grew. Today, it's located in a three-story building in East Sandwich, packed with new and old books, and it's still owned and operated by the Titcomb family. You can find anything from rare collector's items to a large children's section. Snap a photo with the statue of the Colonial man out front, built by the owners! You'll be in good company, as authors such as Alice Hoffman, Henry Winkler, and others have made it a tradition to pose by the statue when they do book signings at the store.

432 MA-6A, East Sandwich, 508-888-5679
titcombsbookshop.com

SHOP
AT THE SANDWICH
ANTIQUES CENTER AND GALLERY

This 5,000-square-foot shop features everything from fine art to furniture, with antiques and accessories for sale from more than 70 dealers. It's fun to browse around, and you never know what will catch your eye on any given day. You can easily spend an hour or more wandering through the large venue, and the staff is super helpful if you are looking for something in particular. If you need a break from the sun or, alternatively, if the weather has driven you inside, this spot will help you while away the time. If you want a peek in advance, check out the shop's robust Instagram page.

131 Rte. 6A, Sandwich, 508-833-3600
sandwichantiquescenter.com

PICK UP
SOME PENNY CANDY
AT THE 1856 COUNTRY STORE

Exactly what you'd want and expect in an old country store—a variety of goods ranging from candy to hardware to toys to jams and anything else you can think of—can be found in this fun shop, which has been owned and operated by the same family since the 1970s. The building's history goes much further back, though; it was built in 1840 as a cranberry harvest storage site. In 1842, it was turned into a shoe store. It changed once again in 1856, this time to a general store, which it has remained.

555 Main St., Centerville, 508-775-1856
1856countrystore.com

DON'T WAIT
FOR A RAINY DAY

A beloved staple in Vineyard Haven since 1973, Rainy Day is a delightful gift shop where you can discover all sorts of items: island-made products such as honey, soaps, and mugs; quirky games and puzzles for adults and kids; beautiful table settings and glassware; and much more. The owners do an excellent job of sourcing items that aren't found in most other island stores, making it a great place to find a locally made souvenir or gift. While items do come and go, recent favorites include the Martha's Vineyard Sea Salt Traveler Three-Pack, made with natural Vineyard sea salt, and custom Martha's Vineyard map socks. This is also one of the few shops on the island that stays open year-round, making it a go-to spot for gifts anytime.

66 Main St., Vineyard Haven, 508-693-1830
rainydaymv.com

GET A SOUVENIR
AT THE MARTHA'S VINEYARD GLASSWORKS

It can be a challenge leaving The Martha's Vineyard Glassworks without a new purchase in hand, but why would you want to? Gorgeous, one-of-a-kind creations are available for purchase, and you never know what might catch your eye. There are two galleries to check out, with rotating pieces from local and Glassworks artists. There is also a viewing space where you can watch glassblowers at their work in the Hot Shop. Among pieces that are usually in stock are the colorful and playful "Fruit Loop" drinking glasses and decorative garden floats, based on the fishing floats used to secure nets. Either or both make for great souvenirs or gifts. Try to buy just one!

683 State Rd., West Tisbury, 508-693-6026
mvglassworks.com

POP INTO
THE BUNCH OF GRAPES BOOKSTORE

This independent, locally owned bookstore in Vineyard Haven has been in business for more than 40 years, and it is known for hosting amazing author events. The store has been in only a few people's hands over the years and is a beloved island institution. The well-stocked shop offers a variety of genres and, like most bookstores, will order anything for you that it doesn't have. Visiting authors, even if just on vacation, will sometimes pop in to sign their books, so you never know if you'll find an autograph as you take a book from the shelf. Another bonus is that the store is open year-round. Pop in to peruse the selection.

23 Main St., Vineyard Haven, 508-693-2291
bunchofgrapes.indielite.org

GET A CUSTOM PIECE
FROM CB STARK JEWELERS

This is the island's go-to jewelry shop and has been for decades. This is the place to come for a gorgeous souvenir of your time on the island, as well as a variety of lovely engagement rings and wedding bands. Many of the handcrafted designs, more than 500 and counting to date, are inspired by the coast, maritime heritage, and distinctive architectural landmarks of Martha's Vineyard. There are two shops you can visit, one open year-round in Vineyard Haven and one open seasonally in Edgartown. The shops can also do antique jewelry restorations, jewelry and watch repair, and engraving.

53A Main St., Vineyard Haven, 508-693-2284
10 Main St., Edgartown, 508-627-1260
cbstark.com

PICK UP A BOOK
AT EDGARTOWN BOOKS

Edgartown Books, another excellent indie bookstore in a central location on Main Street in town, offers two floors of books in all genres, plus a variety of puzzles, games, and gifts, and is also home to the excellent Behind the Bookstore restaurant (which serves amazing cocktails). Happily, it's also open year-round, so you can pick up a book any time and catch a book signing by a local or visiting author. Previous signings have featured renowned authors such as Amor Towles (*The Lincoln Highway*, *A Gentleman in Moscow*) and Edith Blake (*The Making of the Movie Jaws*). Check the shop's Instagram account for updates.

44 Main St., Edgartown, 508-627-8463
edgartownbooks.com

ACQUIRE ITEMS
AT THE ISLAND ALPACA COMPANY

While it's fun to visit the Island Alpaca Company to see the adorable animals, if that's not your thing, you should stop by anyway for the farm's excellent gift shop. The alpacas are bred for their fleece, and in the shop, you'll find a plethora of alpaca-fleece items, including sweaters, mittens, wrist warmers, gloves, toys, dryer balls, scarves, bags, and, of course, alpaca yarn and patterns for making your own creations. In addition, you'll find locally made jewelry, ornaments, and much more. If you'd like to learn how to spin yarn, you can take a two-session introductory workshop.

1 Head of the Pond Rd., Oak Bluffs, 508-693-5554
islandalpaca.com

TAKE A LOOK
AT NANTUCKET LOOMS

If you want to take a little bit of Nantucket home with you, this shop, in business since 1968, can help. You'll find Nantucket cottage-style home furnishings, handwoven textiles, clothing, and accessories galore. With more than 80 local artisans represented at the store, including painters, potters, wood carvers, basket weavers, and jewelry makers, a local design aesthetic is practically guaranteed. And while Nantucket has a reputation as a very pricey island (and it is!), you can find some surprisingly reasonably priced original artwork here. The shop has produced handwoven textiles made from all-natural fibers since it opened its doors. Pick up rugs, throws, blankets, place mats, table runners, kitchen towels, or whatever else you might want in the textile line.

51 Main St., Nantucket, 508-228-1908
nantucketlooms.com

TIP

If you want a customized handwoven item,
Nantucket Looms master weaver Rebecca
Peraner can work with you to create
a one-of-a kind heirloom with the colors,
fibers, and design you like.

BROWSE
AT BLUE BEETLE

Look for the blue convertible Volkswagen Beetle belonging to owner Liz Hughes on Main Street, and you'll know you're in the right place. Inside, the shop showcases clothes, jewelry, gifts, and accessories that portray the "summer lifestyle" of Nantucket. If you need an outfit for a fashionable party that you were just invited to, you'll have plenty of options here. In addition, Nantucket jewelry is a specialty, so you can pick up an island-themed necklace, charm, or bead as a souvenir. The shop is also known for monogramming, so you can get anything from purses to ornaments personalized to your specifications.

12 Main St., Nantucket, 508-228-3227
bluebeetlenantucket.com

MAKE A STOP
AT MADE ON NANTUCKET

With a focus on original artwork from 19 island artists, this gallery/shop, owned and operated by artist Kathleen A. Duncombe for almost 30 years, is a favorite with both residents and visitors. The shop features a large vintage Bakelite jewelry, barware, and kitchenware collection, a draw for many people, along with handwoven items by Karin Sheppard of Island Weaves, Native American jewelry, and much more. In addition, the shop's famous Christmas "Stroll" ornament, which changes every year, is a definite collector's item for many. It's been a symbol of the holidays on the island for about 20 years.

20 Old South Wharf, Nantucket, 508-228-0110
madeonnantucket.net

BUY A BOOK
AT MITCHELL'S BOOK CORNER
OR NANTUCKET BOOKWORKS

If you can't find a book at one of these two island mainstays (which are sister stores), you need to try harder. Mitchell's on Main Street has been in business since 1968, with the most extensive selection of books available about Nantucket, whaling, and the island's genealogy, along with other types of books. Bookworks, which opened in 1972, is just a tad bit younger than Mitchell's, but just as fabulous. It has an apartment called the Second Story Loft available to rent above the shop, which is a dream for book lovers who want to stay permanently.

Mitchell's Book Corner
54 Main St., Nantucket, 508-228-1080

Nantucket Bookworks
25 Broad St., Nantucket, 508-228-4000

nantucketbookpartners.com

ACTIVITIES
BY SEASON

SPRING

Trace a Legacy on the JFK Trail, 93

Don't Wait for a Rainy Day, 122

Buy a Book at Mitchell's Book Corner or Nantucket Bookworks, 132

Stop and Smell the Flowers at the Daffodil Festival, 48

SUMMER

See a Show at the Cape Playhouse, 32

Tap Your Toes at the South Shore Music Circus or Cape Cod Melody Tent, 34

Surf the Waves at Katama/South Beach, 68

Swim at Joseph Sylvia State Beach, 72

Make a Beeline to the Beaches, 80

FALL

Treasure Hunt at Buzzards Bay Antiques, 118

Go Local at the Cape Cod Museum of Art, 94

Go Indie at the MV Film Society, 108

Be Inspired at the Nantucket Shipwreck & Lifesaving Museum, 96

WINTER

Pick Up Some Penny Candy at the 1856 Country Store, 121

Shop at the Sandwich Antiques Center and Gallery, 120

Soak in Some History at Newes from America Pub, 16

Try for a Strike at the Barn, 43

SUGGESTED
ITINERARIES

CLASSIC CAPE COD

Caper at the Cape Cod National Seashore, 65

Cycle the Cape Cod Rail Trail, 54

Adventure with Art's Dune Tours, 40

Take in the Towering Pilgrim Monument and Provincetown Museum, 100

BEACH BUMS

Swim at Joseph Sylvia State Beach, 72

Caper at the Cape Cod National Seashore, 65

Surf the Waves at Katama/South Beach, 68

Make a Beeline to the Beaches, 80

HISTORY BUFFS

Trace a Legacy on the JFK Trail, 93

Learn Island Lore at the Martha's Vineyard Museum, 99

Visit the Museum of African American History, 110

Be Inspired at the Nantucket Shipwreck & Lifesaving Museum, 96

CRAZY FOR SEAFOOD

Down a Dozen at Naked Oyster Bistro, 3

Slurp an Oyster at Topper's, 25

Sate Your Sushi Cravings at Mac's Shack, 8

Get a Lobster Roll at Larsen's Fish Market, 21

FOODIE FANS

BREWS AND MORE

BOOKWORMS

EXCITING EVENTS

Why Toad Hall?

Way back, Kenneth Graham wrote a great children's book called *The Wind In The Willows*. The characters were all animals. The main character was Toad, who was a fairly wealthy landowner in England in the 1890's. He became fascinated with the new motor cars. His manor house was Toad Hall. Bill has the same fascination today. And, that's why this is called Toad Hall. And that's why there are frogs in every car. In honor of Mr. Toad himself.

Why Minuteman Racing?

Bill used to race Datsuns, a 240Z in C Production and a 510 in B Sedan in SCCA back in the 1970's. He lived on Minuteman Road in Hingham, Mass. at the time, and called the Race Team MINUTEMAN RACING.

He just kinda got in the habit of putting MINUTEMAN RACING decals on even his street cars. He never really grew up, and does that to this day, even to the Bentley.

How Did This Collection Start?

Bill always had a couple of cars, but by 1995 he was up to about 5. Then it just kept going. He built a 3 car shed, then a 2 car shed and expanded it to 4 cars. Bought more cars, and then more sheds. He bought around 3-5 a year up 'til 2000. Then his folk's estate was settled, their house sold, and as stocks didn't look that great, he bought around 20 cars. The count is up to around 58 (in 2003). Most were red to begin with, but a dozen or so were painted red.

INDEX